COMMUNION

GREY B. BROWN

Communion

ISBN: 9798899330186 (Paperback)
Library of Congress Control Number: 2026902634
Cover Design: Erin Mann
Book Design: Patrick Holt
Cover photo by Alan Dehmer, woodsedge.net
Author photo by Sally Austin

Printed in the United States of America.
First printing 2026.

Redhawk Publications
The Catawba Valley Community College Press
2550 Hwy 70 SE
Hickory, NC 28602
https://redhawkpublications.com

Dedicated to my mom and my dad,
Elizabeth Grey Harper and James Claud Brown

communion:

the sharing or exchange of intimate thoughts and feelings, especially when the exchange is on a mental or spiritual level

Contents

I

II

III

Backseat

You are sprawled along the backseat,
(one of the many wonderful things
you can't do anymore),
to be so calm, watching trees fly,
and the miles sliding like good rope
between your father's hands.

Long distance over,
you and your parents head for home,
your mother quiet, the games over,
the radio done. The wheels
sway you to sleep, the car like one big
hammock, there on the backroads
safe on the edge of your hometown,
forever almost there.

I Set the Table Before Dinner

I have been taught
the correct order of things,
linen tablecloth,
embroidered napkins,
place settings.

My older sister,
the teaspoon,
long-necked and elegant
lies just above the plate,
crossing the rest of us.

My brother, the salad fork
with crew cut tines is too eager
with my father, the tall fork,
at his side.

My mother, the knife,
is gleaming and me
I place last,
the dessert spoon
small and shallow.

At Morning Break

The teacher unfurls
sheets of drawing paper
to settle lightly before us.
I love the way one piece
blankets my desk.

I push crayons across
and squint at my marks
to see the mountains
and valleys of color.

Sometimes I draw villages
to help me feel at home:
teepees and campfires,
friendly faces, long black hair
like my own, many mothers
in every scene, children
running with dogs,
everyone decorated
with feathers.

Other times
I draw a line along the edge
of my paper and fill the entire space
with smaller and smaller squares
until I reach the middle,
safe again.

Only Son

I wanted everything he had
the compass dangling from cargo shorts,
the pocketknife. I wanted flannel,
a hat with ear flaps.

I wanted the tree house,
the weekends building,
the hammering and the nails.
My father taught him
bird calls, how to whistle.

Once they traveled to Canada,
to the World's Fair,
just the two of them
with a mattress wedged
into the station wagon,
the magic of maps
and special travel snacks.

Their present to me,
a *Canadian* doll,
pudge-faced,
blue eyes and dressed
like any other baby.
I hated her
just as much as I hated other dolls.

My father said
he could always tell
when his son was happy,
just by the way he whistled.

Shoreline

I dropped my beach ball
and the wind took it out to sea.
I stood watching it spin,
touching down to the crest of a wave,
then lifting up again,
happier than it had been
with me. I was not sad to lose it.

Two men in bright trunks
went dashing, kicking into the sea.
Anyone could tell they were swimmers,
their long arms cartwheeling.
When they looked back to me,
I turned away.

My ball tossed freely
beyond their reach.
They swam back
and trotted right up to me,
crouching too closely,
patting my head,
dripping in apology.

Communion

As a child
I sat with my cat
both of us observing
the world beneath the matted grass,
patch by patch
to see what might cross,
a black widow, a roly-poly,
a worm snake,

hunched in concentration,
not allowing our gaze
to wander.
The trees, towering above us,
leaned in as well
and we enjoyed their company
as we enjoyed ourselves.

Merry-Go-Round

I do not want to see
my childless aunt
in her everyday gray
all-weather raincoat,
her lips pursed,
her fingers trilling the air
each time I pass.

I stand in the stirrups
because she hates that.
Here on my horse,
she cannot hold my hand
the way she insists.
She is too timid
to climb onto the rickety carousel,
too stiff to throw a leg over.

I like to imagine my mother there
on a stallion beside me,
stylish in her crisp shirtdress,
and espadrilles, her lips
bright red, sitting tall
in the saddle, singing along,
Pop goes the weasel,
swinging out to take aim
pop, pop
pop.

My mother who now lives
in pajamas, too sick
to leave the house.
She married my father
just for the way he danced,
the man she now hates
for still dancing.

My aunt is always ready
to take me to the park, the pool,
a snack waiting
on the backseat beside me.
She brings banana bread,
washes our clothes,
then sneaks around
to make the beds.
I hate my aunt for being
the only chance I have.

Costume

I am five, maybe six,
and my mother
is taking pictures of me
in my costume.
I stand statue still
before the hearth,
sneakers on,
plastic pumpkin in hand,
ready.

I have chosen a princess dress
and a witch hat.
I like the way I look in purple
and pink, but I need the hat.

My teenage brother walks by
and announces that
I cannot be both
a princess and a witch.
Because of the hat
I am bold and remind him
that he is too old for Halloween
and that no matter what I am,
witch, princess or sister,
he will not be getting candy.

My mother does not say a word
but cocks an eyebrow
the way she does
when she is reading a good book.
Then, as a princess,
I bow.

Cat Eyed

No one had any idea,
certainly not the second-grade teacher
who saw me squinting
and called me *cry baby*
until I cried.

I craned out over my school desk,
straining to see what others saw,
begging to know which words to copy
from the glaze of chalkboard letters.

Call it benign neglect,
call it being the fifth born,
no one saw how hard
I worked to see.

The ophthalmologist
arrived at our school,
very matter of fact,
unrolled his chart
and seated us one by one.
When it came to me,
the small man touched his brow
and whistled.

On the way home
from the eye doctor,
I sported tortoise shell,
cat-eyed glasses,
face pressed to the window,
startling my family
shouting *Stop!*
at every corner,
murmuring, *The leaves,*
the leaves, the leaves.

Cursive

Your fingers are sore from oversized pencils,
the heel of your hand dark with lead,
as you learn the tightness of print.

You grow to love crisp letters,
the measured space between,
the ease of discipline.

But now, third grade and new letters swim
white on green above the chalkboard.
They look lazy, flirtatious with their curls

carelessly dangling empty loops
and when your teacher connects them,
they fall into one another's laps

or crawl onto each other's backs
tangling until
no one can decipher them.

This is letters gone bad, letters misbehaving,
and you yearn for the no-nonsense of print.
Even worse, you no longer own a desk,

but work at tables in groups
where the boys make fun of your drawings
and call you weird.

In truth, you never master the curves
though you let your letters lean a bit,
but for the most part they remain

straight, upright,
perhaps at times
lightly holding hands.

The Scots

My great aunts
live ditch-bound in the county,
outbuildings sagging,
a neon Budweiser always lit.

I like their whistling kettle
and the tea cakes,
the clutter, their chatter,
the sofa on the porch,

their jokes that make no sense
but keep my mother laughing.
I admire most their birdhouses,
dangling white gourds

twirling above forgotten fields,
dry, empty globes
suspended six in a row,
angled against the sky,

unlikely totems,
livelier than any cross,
eyeless, their round mouths
open, wordless, calling.

Each Easter Sunday

my mother forgave
all Christian hypocrites
and joined the throng,

her woven,
wide brimmed hat,
her hand tailored A-line dress,

slender feet
in strappy sandals.
She was a head taller

than the preacher's wife
who wore (God help us)
a mint green pantsuit.

They say we dress
for church so that God
will see us at our best

and bless us.
My mother did not pine
for God's eyes.

She paraded
for the Sunday school teachers,
Bible study leaders,

despite and in spite
of their judgement.

Smile!

Because her sister drove,
my mother, too anxious to drive,
always had a ride.
Because my father gave her money
my mother, who never worked,
could always buy.

Because my aunt led me
to Woolworths for popcorn and a Coke,
my mother crossed the tracks,
hoofed it two blocks,
circled back,
the fifth tucked neatly in her bag.

I forgive my mother
(her first drink had been prescribed)
and my father,
he did what he could
to keep her alive.

But I work each day
to forgive the aunt
who always reminded me
to smile.

Second Coming

In my grandmother's house,
Jesus showed up in unusual places.
In the hall, he kindly held a thermometer.
With wavy brown hair, blue eyes shining,
he peered down from the calendar.
In the kitchen, a Jesus postcard
(*Wish you were here*!) prayed over crates
of Dr. Pepper, one hundred
and forty-four bottles,
unopened, crusted in dust.

As my grandmother told it,
that Dr. Pepper man
came out of nowhere, stepped
right up on her porch
and shook her hand. He said
he would give her a silver dollar
for every bottle she had.
To her dismay she did not have a single one.
You could beg all day in that house
and not even Jesus
could give you a sip.

TV Was Not Always

There was only one
in every home,
you rarely watched it alone.

To watch a favorite show
you had to consult
a printed guide, know

the date and time
and pay attention
because when it began

it ran and was done,
no streaming, no taping,
no rewind. You watched

and then waited
seven days and seven nights
for your show to be new again.

It was best to be prepared
with snacks and milk
or better yet

with fancy TV dinners
on special TV trays.
At midnight,

The Star-Spangled Banner played,
the flag waved
while all the animals

and all the people huddled
behind a humming,
patterned screen.

Lassie Theme: *The Whistle Tune*

Every week at the end of the show,
after she pulled Timmy from the well,
or saved the bay mare from the burning stall,
Lassie waited alone
in a clearing of trees,
while someone off-screen
whistled a mournful tune
and even you at six years old
knew she could not last.

She would be crushed
by the John Deere
or her liver would fail,
or worse, some neighbor,
tired of her perfection,
would poison her.

And as the credits streamed,
both you and Lassie waited
until the moment
when she lifted her right paw
to say she saw you.

Swim Lessons, Holiday Inn, Highway 301

My mother is poolside
under a faded umbrella.
She is wearing a Panama hat
to hide her limp gray hair,
dark sunglasses
and a dry one-piece.
She sits alone
with her whiskey in a thermos
away from the shiny moms.

Today, we learn to dive.
The teacher shows us how to kneel
to press our palms together,
as if in prayer, to stretch that prayer
out over the water. If we aim our fingers,
our bodies will follow.
I plunge into prayers unanswered,
knocking pool bottom,
and come up gagging.

My mother wobbles to the edge
and somehow balances to squat,
sweating in her effort, her hands
shaking. I lean against her
and cover my head with my towel
as my friends arch, dive,
rise up from deep water.

Skyview Skateland

Around the rink, skaters glide,
lights dimmed for *Couple,*
Couples Only Skate.
My father is skating with a woman,
not my mother who never comes.

My father and this woman,
tall and pretty, glide in
and out of view,
to the back of the shadowy rink,
then sailing towards me again, smiling.

The spinning mirror ball throws
rainbows along their path,
Unchained Melody spurs them on.
He gently guides her, pressing
his palm to the small of her back.
They turn to skate backwards,
turn effortlessly again.

My father is a master skater
and volunteers to teach anyone,
but selects this same woman
for couples' skate, week after week.

From the old auditorium seats
that circle the rink,
I watch them, hypnotized,
enjoying their grace and skill,
not thinking of my mother,
not thinking at all.

Star-Studded Birthday

July 20th, 1969

The day I turn ten is the day
of the first moon landing.
My mother and I know this
(we love the moon)
but she is ill,
too ill for a party.

At my aunt's house,
I plan to watch the event,
but my aunt laughs,
tells me to forget about that hooey,
the latest conspiracy,
just another communist plot.

I think of the party
my mother had planned,
the glittery invitations,
the moon cake with green icing,
Pin the Ring on Saturn,
Don't Drop the Asteroid.

Alone before the box TV,
I wait for the big event,
the astronauts waving,
planting the flag in my name,
singing *Happy Birthday*
just as my mother had promised.

George's Garden

Before the illness, my aunt's husband had gardened,
lain flagstones winding from garage to screened-in porch,
planted azalea mazes, daffodils, my favorite cup and saucer tree.
Never wanting children, this garden was his progeny.

After his illness, I was free to pick any flower,
to water and prune, to sprawl on moss for hours,
the leaves singing only to me.

I loved to roam his forbidden potting shed,
trowels and forks in obedient rows,
terracotta pots upturned, his projects still waiting.
He could no longer walk, no longer catch me.

Daytime, he sat in a chair in the den,
unable to speak, his eyes following me.
I knew not to wander too close
though I liked to stand a safe distance, challenging.

Once, a misstep and I teetered,
my arm falling on his.
He grabbed me lightning quick,
even his weak hand a tight grip
and my aunt called, *George, George,*
you have to let her go,
but his eyes never veered from mine,
his grip so slow to release
a blooming bruise.

First Wedding

My sister's wedding was,
I learned later,
a shotgun wedding
in a town across the state line
where marriage could be had
in no time, shop and go,
quick stop.
In the chapel with linoleum tiles,
folding chairs and fluorescent lights,
I fingered the rice tucked
in my pocket,
remembering weddings
from TV.

I tossed the rice,
my sister hissed,
and a man in a dark suit
came quickly
wagging his finger,
pointing to the grains
now trapped in the grooves
of the black mat that curved
from sliding glass doors
to marriage.

I Come to the Garden Alone

Even with a beard,
Jesus was prettier
than I would ever be—
fresh blue eyes,
unblemished skin,
high cheekbones,
the light playing
on his chestnut hair.
Women who taught Sunday school,
who chaperoned listless youth,
single women and wives,
young and old, all longed
to be cradled in his arms.
Jesus loved these women most.
In the church kitchen,
he sat on the counter,
dangling sandaled feet
while they measured his blood
into tiny cups,
arranging his flesh on doilies.
The older women at church,
rotund pigeons with the best intentions,
their hymnals propped
on the shelf of their bosoms,
stood still and straight,
singing and hardly blushing—

And he walks with me
And he talks with me
And he tells me I am his own.
And the joy we share
As we tarry there,
None other has ever known

Public Swimming Pool, 1970

Beyond the fence, on bright concrete
girls spread patterned beach towels,
tune transistor radios,

check out one another's dance moves.
The white girls set out iodine
and baby oil. They too will be brown

by summer's end.
The Black girls care for their hair,
avoid splashing, bright swim caps

like water lilies bobbing on the water.
The boys wrestle and jack-knife
from the high dive.

Around the pool they all swagger,
Black and white keeping an eye
on each other and the other.

I long to show off my new bathing suit,
my cannonball, but my father says
I will not swim with *Blacks.*

The girl who lives behind me
swims every day with her teenage sister.
They bike, wearing only their suits,

towels caped around their shoulders
like superheroes. They spread
their arms like wings.

The YMCA

John, tall, dark, youth director
played a mean game of keep away
and taught our young bodies to dive.
We hugged the edge of the trampoline
while he twirled above.
He called us his girls,
gave us piggyback rides.

One day after a lesson in the breaststroke,
Sally pulled me to the locker room floor
and straddled my waist, dangling a bag of makeup
I had never seen before.

I did not resist as she blushed my cheeks,
curled my lashes. She nodded
and bent to kiss me
not long, but enough
before I pushed her off,
both of us laughing,
my eyes rimmed with kohl,
Sally gaining a head start
to find him

Summer Morning

Sometimes I wake
as the girl with blond hair

and tall legs in my airy, upstairs
bedroom, the windows open to spring,

the smell of cut grass
and willow shadows dancing.

And it is Saturday, always Saturday,
and my family

is downstairs packing a picnic,
just waiting for me to join them

for something wonderful
we will do on that day,

a day without fighting,
without anyone being drunk

without "God damn it to hell,"
this morning that does not need

to lean on wishes or prayers.
Like other families we will squabble,

a tiff about taking turns,
but nothing that will ever

scar us. My mother, suddenly young,
will not chain smoke in our station wagon

and my father will not get lost again,
his anger shuttered till the shouting,

his open palm springing
over the front seat to cuff us.

And my brother will not
lean in to remind me

that I still cannot ride
a two-wheel bike,

noting I will never grow,
that my head still

outsizes my body,
will not whisper stupid *waterhead.*

Intersection

My mother no longer sits to eat,
stands at the sink,
enjoying the spin-sucking strength
of the new disposal.

My father dines at the table,
sporting a buttermilk mustache,
forking in canned carrots and corn,
saying, *Honey, this sure is good.*

He slips a twenty
into her grocery jar,
pats his pocket
like a banker, satisfied.

He mugs for the mirror,
pecks her cheek
as he leaves for a beautician
in a nearby town.

She eases into the rhythm
of solitude, relieved
to be done with the sticky skin
of tolerance and good behavior.

In a wingback chair
she swirls her glass, sunlit amber.
She is happy now
should anyone ask.

Burn

She was just rolling me over
in bed after I was asleep.
She must have been making
room to lie down beside me,
cigarette in hand
and she was just too gone
to notice the tip to skin,
to smell the flesh.

She must have paused,
to catch her breath,
her hands heavy on my legs.
It was hard to roll me over,
weight of my sleep and dreaming.

In my dreaming I saw
a ring of fire. I brushed
the flame away,
never woke to the pain.

For weeks of unwanted attention,
the wound at the crook of my knee
was revealed by shorts,
open, oozing,
slow to heal, "needing air,"
gnats gathering
around its humid rim.

Thompson's Greenhouse

In the seedling house,
out of the freezing rain,
it is moist and warm,
the soil trays spread
before me and I am grateful
for this indoor job
on a late February day.

Mr. Thompson has left me
with seeds to sow
and I imagine myself
a fertile goddess,
a young one, age fifteen,
giving birth again and again,
safe from wind and chill.

On slow days, I watch Mrs. Thompson
baby her terrariums, miniature worlds
she towers above, tamping down
tiny palms and ferns, placing pagodas
and bridges, keeper of climate.

Some days I walk around stunned
that someone knows this much,
greenhouses sprawling, thousands
of plants moving from trays to pots
to homes, all synchronized with seasons.

I am short-haired and thin,
breastless and muscled.
Most days I wear my overalls.
The older women say
Thank you, young man
as I haul trees to their cars,
dogwood, redbud, tulip magnolia.

Don't Be So Serious

they said and I really was,
wanting the *Three Stooges*
just to cut it out, wanting to know
how anyone ever came back
from being flattened,
knowing that when you run
over a cliff, you can't just
backup and start running again.

Lassie made me anxious,
the high spiteful violin
telling us something bad
was about to happen.
I worried about what happened
when we did not watch,
when Lassie was in heat,
not giving a damn about anyone,
especially not Timmy.

And Disney troubled me.
Did no one else want to know
what happened to all the mothers?
And I never wanted
to be a princess because then
your mother had been dead
a long time and things
were about to get worse.

And the people of the church
who went on and on about the virgin birth.
What if the school nurse
had not told us everything,
what if even God was a dirty old man
and could come down to earth
at any time. He would find us alone
waiting for the bus, or beside a bike
with a loose chain, in the dark
corner of a library and he would
make us do it, right then and there
and there was nothing, not a thing
we could do.

I never trusted spring,
one minute all dogwoods
and daffodils, bunnies and eggs—
the next hammered feet and hands
and a bloody crown,
the horror of drinking blood,
the wafer sucked to soggy flesh.
I never knew how I should feel
about eating chocolate rabbits.
Don't be so serious, they said.

II

Harrison's Dock

If you bike down to the shaded lawns,
turn behind the white columned houses,
jump the curb and duck branches,
pass the totem pole carved by rich boys,
skid down the hill,
swerving just before the river,
you can be there in ten minutes,
a private dock,
No Trespassing Allowed.

This is the place to consider
your mother's death,
your older brother's contempt,
the daughters of doctors and lawyers
who call your father white trash
and taunt you with their college plans.
Your heart clenched,
you aren't really sad
or angry, you are magnified.

You will go beyond this place,
rising above the tented carousel,
up over tobacco fields,
till the trees wave goodbye
and the water tower winks.

I Hate October

I just seem to lose family and friends
as the light angles down—
my grandmother to colon cancer,
the neighbor's daughter
who just overdosed,
my dearest friend tucked in a shawl,
the book falling from his hand.
They all seem to let go,
as daylight wanes
and a cool hand disturbs the earth.

I talk more to my mother
at this time of year,
but she is of little help,
so bad at living herself,
her drinking and smoking.

She passed in the fall
of her fifty-ninth year.
She was an ardent fan
of witches and ghosts,
pumpkins and gourds.
I still decorate for her
trying to do my best
with the darkness.

Graveside

As they lower my aunt
into the ground.
this burbling, flickering boy
wheels up on his banana bike.
With his loud squeaks and clicks,
he might be speaking in tongues
but probably isn't,
one word here and there,
then a winding chant.
He flares his hands
against the sun, eyes squinting
to watch their dance.
I step away from the silent crowd
closer to this boy,
the only one who makes sense to me
on this thin rim between life and after.

After the Service

In truth, this time is never
about the dead,
but rather for kith and kin,
in-laws compensating
with sagging paper plates,
antsy descendants
waiting for the will.

Now, the seasoned matriarchs
step from the kitchen, untying aprons
to reveal their Sunday best,
wiping their soft brows,
women who still wear skirts
and believe in perms.

After second helpings of spiral ham,
the caramel cake parades in,
the icing delicately boiled:
too little handiwork and the sugar
slides off in pools,
too much and it bristles into spears.

Noted only by the family cat,
the deceased finds her way
in and out of books, dims
the chandelier, then skims
the sitting room, before
settling into new forms:
the curve of an eyelash, fallen,
the forgotten ringtone,
a collective consciousness
carried by ants

Ancestry

When we were little,
our father said his father
left his mother
to return to Ireland.

My father said
he understood
and it made me
love the country,

though in the end,
I wasn't Irish.
Once my sister
sent him a blank book
to fill in his ancestry.

My father sent it back blank.
Later we learned
there was no romantic
return to the homeland,

just a fatherly man,
who cut hair downtown,
and who cut
my father's hair for free.

How Sweet the Sound

Retired to Florida, my father
witnesses the Challenger explosion,
then drives thirty miles
before he realizes
he has no idea
where he is going.

A week later,
I walk with him
along the beach
at Cape Canaveral
as divers in wetsuits
comb the surf for remains.

My father is falling
into himself, smaller
each time I see him.

In faded, baggy trunks
he huffs along the sand,
a steady pace, humming
his favorite, *Amazing Grace,*
casting his net
for each soul passing.

Family Plot

Once on a cruise,
my mother spent the week
not letting my father find her.
Behind a book,
hunkered in a deck chair,
she would see him coming
and dash starboard
then dash again if need be.

She thought him ridiculous
disco dancing at 70,
his shorts and tube socks.
Why couldn't he just read?
His second wife
insisted on his cremation
and I imagined my father
dancing into flames.

Now my mother
rolls alone under
the grass and plastic flowers
of a double plot, bought
too soon.

She draws the soil
up under her chin
but still does not miss him.
She wonders what will happen
to the space beside her.
She would not mind
if someone else moved in
perhaps someone sensible,
someone who reads.

The Remaining Deacons Discuss Selling the Church

The silver candle holders
should bring a pretty penny
and then there's the altar,
cherry inlay and all.

We must pay to remove
the baptismal pool. They prefer
fire. They are not happy
with the pews, frayed cushions
and scuffed wood from children
too rough for Sunday School.
They'd rather have folding chairs,
seats wheezing during silent prayer.

Bob will take the elder's table
for a workbench. He will pray
each time before he hammers.
We'll donate the collection plates,
that in the end, were empty anyway.
They don't realize that the pulpit
does not convey. They'll arrive
to find a jagged space
a bad tooth might leave behind.

The new congregation
will have a praise band
and a smoke machine.
They have no idea
how iffy old wiring can be.
Imagine loud guitars, drums,
bass thumping, then the fuses will blow.
Even so, they will keep singing
and clapping, even in darkness
they will keep praising.

To My Sister

At what point
did you say goodbye?
You still have a child,

but never again
a daughter,
the two of you

in a California hotel,
after the mastectomy.
Did your own breasts

strain at the sight?
The little girl you dressed
in plaid skirts and tights,

your matching berets—
did you ever waver
in support,

sorting the drugs
to let whiskers appear
and her voice grow deep?

He kept some softness
at least for a while.
You always accepted him

even as you dulled
in his disdain.
Now, he never calls

except for money,
or to say he is in jail.
Still, you never imagined

he would twist
childhood memories
into trauma and lies.

At your lake cabin
I find a photo of my niece, gone
but not deceased,

floating in some in-between,
dressed in black,
skateboard tough

with studs and chains,
her strong arms
still wrapped around you.

Waiting for Swifts

When we danced,
the neighbors complained,
striking a broom handle
against their ceiling—
Les Americans!

They chided us
for never polishing
our share of the stairs.
We would find them
heads together, clucking,
poking at our sacks
of curbside trash.

Even in our own apartment,
we were imposters,
making do with two burners,
dreaming of showers,
waiting for the BBC.
Bare plaster walls resented
our futon, our folding chairs,
our tasteless table lamps.

But the sky was ours,
a low, motionless gray.
At day's end, we sat together,
before the casement window,
its doors spread open like wings,
our bare feet propped
on a generous sill.

We wanted wine
but had so little money.
We settled for swifts,
shape shifters, their spirals
twisting twilight to night,
known for screaming parties,
able to roost in midair,
mating on the wing.

Oh, Man

When exasperated,
I might wring my hands,
sigh and say,
Man, but which man
in particular?

Do I have a specific
man in mind, taller
than myself and broader,
a blank face? A ski mask
comes to mind.

Which might lead us
to the man who breaks in at night.
I live alone,
often forget to lock the door
and in the morning
I stare at the latch unlatched,
thinking, "Man."

Tell me, when you think
of someone breaking into your home,
do you think woman or man?
Who do you imagine
scaling your wall,
searching the windowsill,
arm reaching in?

Frankly, if I saw a woman
my first thought would be
that maybe she needed help,
was running for her life,
had had enough, finally.

Do you know why
we never take elevators
alone? Honed to footsteps
in any parking deck,
we clench our fists,
keys jutting from our knuckles,
poor claws of defense.

Maybe it is the man with great power,
the tax man, the man from the bank
when the payments lapse.
Maybe it is
the state trooper pulling us over
at night, the policeman,
any man, anywhere
when we are upset
to the point of confusion,
no longer making sense,
wielding our flimsy shield of anger.

Or is it a man like God?
Or maybe it is God,
the god who gives
and takes by whim,
the one who people say
will never give us
more than we can handle,
but then rears back,
thunderbolt in hand
and does anyway.
That man.

Our House So Beautiful

We are in the sandbox
when the car pulls up
squarely before our house,
a car we do not recognize,
a man we do not know.

He steps to the curb,
taking photographs.
I stand trying
to look larger than I am
and question him.

He says he is from the bank
and steps onto our lawn,
jutting his chin towards our door.
My daughter is crouching
behind me, so I tell her—

Our house is so beautiful
this man just had to stop
to take pictures.
She brightens, suggests
that we pose, and so we do.

On Belief

My daughter learns of constellations,
the unfinished dot-to-dot
of Andromeda and Cassiopeia,

the poor mother and baby bears
headless, missing paws.
She dreams of planets

and their rings,
adoring moons
that spin and sing.

Stargazing, we find our way
to a dark, empty field
to view the comet.

My daughter imagines
bold strokes, a ball of light
with a vivid, streaming tail,

cartoon crisp and lively colored.
But she finds only
a blurred hairball of dust and ice.

more chaos than divine creation,
at best, the whorled thumbprint
of some god, preoccupied.

Before School Breakdown

We are walking on eggshells,
then breaking eggs,
mucking our way
through the viscous whites,
the yolk like a sun
beginning to fall,
and we drown
while burning.

First the medication works,
and she is clear,
the girl I know,
the girl who holds my hand,
and then doesn't.
Or something,
some scent, some sound
memory bent,
some moment
without routine
trips her.

One minute, she is
heading out the door,
backpack in hand
and then she is on the floor
and I am holding her
down away from the knives
because she wants
to end this. Finally
she sags to my chest
and we lean back
against the cabinets
and I begin counting again.

Ugly Fruit

I drive around behind
the grocery store
as I make a point to do.

There is food to be found there
like racks of cinnamon bread,
still wrapped, just a little mold,

bananas, just a little brown.
This time I spot a grocery cart
with sagging pumpkins,

jostled one on another
like kids crowded
onto a rickety carnival ride.

I know how proud pumpkins
can look lined up
on their seasonal stands,

promising pies,
aspiring to be jack-o-lanterns,
and then there were these guys.

At first, I dismissed them
thinking I could not
but then I kept thinking

how bad could they be?
It takes so little
to be tossed out these days.

I thought of those pumpkins
as I walked my dog
and imagined one roasting

my home filled with the scent,
pumpkin muffins, pumpkin soup.
So, I drove back and sure enough

beneath the rot, there was one
with just a spot on its bottom.
I carried it back,

composted the pulp,
set aside seeds for toasting,
brushed the halves with olive oil,

garden rosemary, coarse salt,
its roasted, unspoiled flesh
tender and forgiving.

Parisian Market, An Honest Place

Here, you might stand
shoulder to shoulder
with a dangling boar
ripening on its hook,
knowing that horses
can be ground into patties.

One shopper orders a rabbit
and the butcher obliges,
removing the head
to slip the skin up
over the shoulders like a child
pulling off pajamas,
Skin the cat, my mother always said.

There is a boy here now
and he holds his father's hand
patiently waiting. The butcher
pauses to place the severed head
over his thumb and then
dances it along the counter,
to both father and son's delight,
a meaty puppet
leaping and dancing.

You watch too, no longer amazed,
you only turn away
when the bloody head
starts singing.

Sincerely

In my late fifties
I cut off my hair.
My daughter says
I am edgy.
I am cutting away the perms,
dyed locks,
my instinct to please.

I am cutting off *yes*
when I mean *no*.
I am cutting away
liking his music
when I really don't
away from still listening,
when I no longer care.

I am cutting off
the expectation
that I might find that someone,
and that if I did find him,
he would love me.

I am cutting myself
from an old postcard
sent to some
parallel universe,
but never received.

I Keep Writing the Poem

with a nod to Tess Gallagher's I Stop Writing the Poem

Doing laundry,
I keep writing the poem,
because my adult daughter

still lives at home
and has too many clothes.
I wish to be the crone

who no longer folds,
but who writes poems
and prose

in black, permanent marker,
on the underwear I never fold.
Ten years divorced

I keep writing the same poem,
the poem that greets me
each morning from kitchen door,

bent over to-do lists,
the bore hunched, chain smoking,
muttering, forlorn.

Empty Nester

I live alone.
My daughter gives me
a robotic massager

to ease away the stress,
to help me relax,
an awkward, oversized

vibrating harness
with a mini-light show,
revolving nodes beaming red.

At the end of the day,
I pull its shy bulk to me
and we cozy on the couch.

I push the buttons,
drill into the pain,
click warm or warmer,

hard or harder, forward, reverse,
its quiet whir a conversation
long forgotten.

Adult Daughter

The morning after
you leave, your image
still layers the living room,
where you laughed,
where you sat,
spoke quietly of your dying cat.

Now you are back where you belong
and I celebrate your independence,
my success. Still, I am a bit sullen,
wanting more of you.
How well I know not to push
or ask too much.

You and your boyfriend
were climbing into the truck
for the five-hour drive back home,
when you turned to see me,
this gesture that sustains me.

My Daughter Loves Me from a Distance

Each time my daughter travels
she brings me a magnet,
a small token of her love.

Here she loved me in Mexico
with a hand painted heart
in her palm.

Here, Une Frise des Chats
et de Lune, street cats
frolicking under the moon,

Musee de Montmartre,
her love so clear
in October light.

Here lime and turquoise lizards
spangle under the Aruban sun,
tiny toes scattering my love.

My collection on the fridge
by my coffee machine,
I like to retrace her travels

as I brew. After two years,
we are speaking again.
I invite her for dinner

and she hands me the latest
from her second visit to Paris.
When I suggest

we travel together someday,
I cross so many boundaries.
My daughter could leave,

turn cold again, ghost me.
But she simply crosses the room
for her glass of wine,
both her answer and no answer.

She's So Creative

I want someone to stop,
full stop, lean in, to scratch
my painted surface
and keep right on digging.

I survive by doing.
Doing earns my place,
the fifth born, born late,
my siblings soon moved on.

I am redundant and ill-placed.
I need a job, let me help,
hands busy, happy heart
or at least a heart willing

to contain itself.
I know my talk alone
cannot engage you,
no matter my patter.

I am so often spoken over
or around, have waited
too long for the well-timed
arch of the rope before I jump in.

But forget me!
Come, see the tree I planted,
the pot I made, read the poem
I wrote, have some spaghetti,

take these hand-bound books,
this crafted Afghan.
Can't you see
how hard I am trying?

Static

My mama used to call it
a bad nerve day
when the dryer is going
and the radio is talking fast
and anybody is asking me
any little thing
and it all rushes into me
hissing like raw wires
like bad electricity.
I go around
turning off things
dryer mid-cycle
radio mid-sentence,
turn off humming lights
the whining freezer
tapping heater
and still.

Talking Elsewhere, Everywhere

My mother would have been
so set with a cell phone,
everyone assuming
she was laughing with a chum,
sharing a joke,
snapping down the street
cell to ear, sweet talking.

At home,
when she talked to herself,
only family could hear
and we took her chatter
in stride. But at the mall,
along downtown streets,
her constant monologue
gave others pause.
They whispered,
cornered me in the gym
to say they had seen her.

My mother might have opted
for earbuds, tiny angels perched
as she talked to God and the dead,
those folks who were always home.

That's All the Time We Have for Today

Anger management issues,
I whisper to the cat,
when tiny brother dog toddles by
and she lassoes his neck for a ride.

She leans into his twitching ears
and is about to rear back
when she catches me watching,
checks herself and begins
a leisurely bath.

There is little hope for this cat.
She killed her therapist, a mouse
who worked with her remotely
from behind the fridge.
These kitchen talks went late
into the night as both struggled
with boundaries.

Like too many therapists,
the mouse imagined
they had made
much more progress
than they ever might.

No Need to Stall with Adderall

with an appreciation for Charlotte Perkins Gilman

I carry my head.
How I chortle!
I am all the bubble words
at once, *ebullient,*
effervescent, loquacious,
chipper than Dale,
my whole body wagging,
zing, zing, zing
and every other
onomatopoeia.

Each workday,
white rabbit dashing,
down a slippery slide
before I scurry home
to clean, so much to do,
do, do. I organize the
organized. I alphabetize.

I feel my self-self
crawling somewhere behind
the fuzzy wallpaper,
but chemistry keeps
that woman trapped
and I plow on,
skipping meals,
chiseled to a fine point,
becoming the answer.

Do You Dream of Flying?

Sometimes I dare myself
to stretch out in air,
kicking my legs back
never certain if this still works.

Low to the ground, my arms dragging,
I must keep remembering
I can do this.

Once I am ceiling height, I wait
for an open window or door.
Sometimes I circle for hours.

Outside I must remember
quadratic equations,
and weigh their formulas
against distance and stamina.

I watch for power lines,
sudden billboards.
None of this is easy or freeing.

Sometimes I do not care
if people are watching
because even

with my halting gait, my face
twisted in concentration,
I am still flying.

Holly and Hills

To say *suicide*,
or to say more softly
suicidal ideation,
is to say farewell
to the brightly lit waiting room,
as the rest remain:
the broken shoulder,
the child with fever,
the man awkwardly asleep,
the woman who approaches
the front desk again,
her voice steadily rising.

You leave through a separate door,
a door you have never seen.
The policeman who waits
is merely protocol.
He shows you to a room,
hands you a gown
and waits outside.
The room is tight,
smaller than a dressing room
with a single chair as though
one might sit there.
Someone taps on the door
reminding you to remove
jewelry as well.

The policeman takes your wallet,
your clothes, your phone
and leads you down
a hall without windows
even farther away
from the other patients
who now lie on gurneys
with blankets and pillows,
fruit juice, an IV drip.

The elevator sinks
to the floor beneath the floor.
The unit is small,
nurses and staff behind glass.
One takes your belongings
to an everyday locker
and keeps the key.

She leaves you in a room
a fleshy shade of pink,
the corners rounded,
the furniture smooth
and solid, easy to clean,
too awkward to move,
too heavy to heave.

The door to each patient room
must remain open, so you watch
as the mother comforts her son,
as the homeless man is released,
as a nurse changes wet bed sheets.

This is not the place,
this is the place between
and the rules have changed.
It will be days before a single bed
opens someplace across the state,
second-rate with low-wage workers,
some place with a snip of nature in its name,
holly and hills, trees, evergreens.

Behind the Back Wings of the Hospital

after William Carlos Williams

Behind the back wings of the hospital
abundance abounds, dumpster brimming,
black bags spilling to concrete.

The squirrels take turns atop the quivering mass,
slash to accommodate slender paws.
Crows who will not sully themselves with actual crime,

wait to reap scattered rewards.
With each squirrel's dash they spring skyward
where they hover and shrug

before strutting again like deacons, full of desire.
Now one squirrel wiggles into the bag,
coquettishly peeking out, sporting a black plastic collar.

How this foolishness
must strain the neighborhood,
idiot clowns with handy claws

while the serious still wait with sharpened beaks.
Wrens and finches skirt the scene,
cheering one team, then the other.

Now the squirrels are poking in and out
of the widening gash, two or three
at a frenzied pace, till this ripe piñata

finally spills forth
for special guests and, yes,
for all the uninvited.

Funny How Things Happen

In a vast hospital catacomb,
my office ends up
on the same hall
as psychiatric emergency.

The door to the unit
is solid. Office clerks
crack jokes as they pass,
darting to the peephole
especially when someone
is keening.

As I head to lunch,
a new patient arrives
in handcuffs shuffling
in a cluster of nurses
and cops who quip,
flirt, catch up
with each other.

Some mornings,
this hallway to my office
is lined with rubber furniture
waiting to be cleaned,
there—the square unyielding seat
where I propped myself awake,
the bare mattress
where I fought to sleep.

Tattoo

I

We gathered our ribbons,
blue for depression,
(perfect, don't you think?),

blinking red for ADHD,
bright green flashing for OCD.
We planned our awareness campaign

for February, the shortest month.
We would have a parade,
the narcissist leading the way.

But we needed a t-shirt.
We considered *Schizophrenia Survivor*
but it did not have the right ring,

or rather, it would not stop ringing.
We discussed *Bipolar Warriors*
Some Days and on the back,

Other Days Not So Much.
We tossed around
We Can Beat Depression

in giant letters and in letters
too small to read
Assisted by Suicide.

II

I want a shirt that admits
none of us ever really survive,
but we get by,

a shirt that lists daily warriors
compensating, those spinning
and flapping and stimming,

those troubled in mind,
mumbling, stumbling,
the haunted artists,

compulsive composers,
poets and playwrights,
those who see in pictures,

shy scientists still misunderstood,
those quiet wizards in IT,
the boy who stays alone

by the playground fence,
all the uninvited.
I want a shirt so graphic

the ink covers the inside-out
as well. I will keep listing
and printing and will not end

at a mere shirt's tail.
I will keep witnessing,
writing up and down

my legs, have someone
scrawl across my back.
I will shave my head

for new space until I stand
a full body tattoo,
testifying.

Acknowledgments

Immense thanks to the Black Socks poets, Ralph Earle, Paul Jones, Debra Kaufman, Gary Phillips, Maura High, Jan Harrington, Florence Nash, and Liza Wolff for their unapologetic and brilliant critique of these poems, and to Dave Caserio, Maura High, and Debra Kaufman for reading the manuscript and providing their notes. Thanks to Jan Freeman for her close reading and revision. Appreciation to the editors who published some of these poems, sometimes under different titles. Thanks to Redhawk for their encouragement and support. Also, thanks to Andrea Selch, nudge, nudge, wink, wink. As always, thanks to Nona, my sometimes muse.

I am grateful to these for publishing these poems in their journals:

Atlanta Review
Ugly Fruit

Cave Wall
Swimming Lessons

Cold Mountain Review
Our House So Beautiful
Parisian Market, an Honest Place

Dead Mule Society of Southern Literature
My First Wedding
Second Coming

Kakalak
Cursive
Don't Be So Serious (nominated for Pushcart)

Ley Lines
Holly and Hills (under the title *Psych ER*)
Tattoo

Litmosphere: Journal of Charlotte Lit
Waiting for Swifts

Red Headed Stepchild
Static

Tar River Poetry
Family Plot

They Wrote Us a Poem Volume 10
Behind the Back Wings of the Hospital

Triggerfish Review
The Scots (published as *Black Irish*)
Merry-Go-Round
Talking Elsewhere, Anywhere

Redheaded Stepchild
Psychiatric ER
Tattoo

About the Author

Grey Brown is a poet and ceramics artist living in Chapel Hill, NC. This is her second full-length manuscript in addition to *What It Takes* and the chapbooks, *Staying In* and *When They Tell Me.* Her poems have been published in numerous journals, including Tar River Poetry, Greensboro Review, Atlantic, Cave Wall, and others. Grey received her master's in English from New York University. She is the founder of the Literary Arts Program of the Health Arts Network at Duke and served as director for 25 years. She lives with her cat, her sometimes muse.

Other books by Grey Brown

Staying In
When They Tell Me
What It Takes

www.ingramcontent.com/pod-product-compliance
Lightning Source LLC
LaVergne TN
LVHW010628100826
845148LV00014B/3153

* 9 7 9 8 8 9 9 3 3 0 1 8 6 *